Kateri of the Mohawks
Coloring Book

This is her story, written by Mary Fabyan Windeatt
With pictures for you to color, drawn by Gedge Harmon

This book belongs to

_____

The pictures in this book can be colored with crayons, markers or water colors.

Copyright©2017 St. Jerome Library Press

All Rights Reserved.

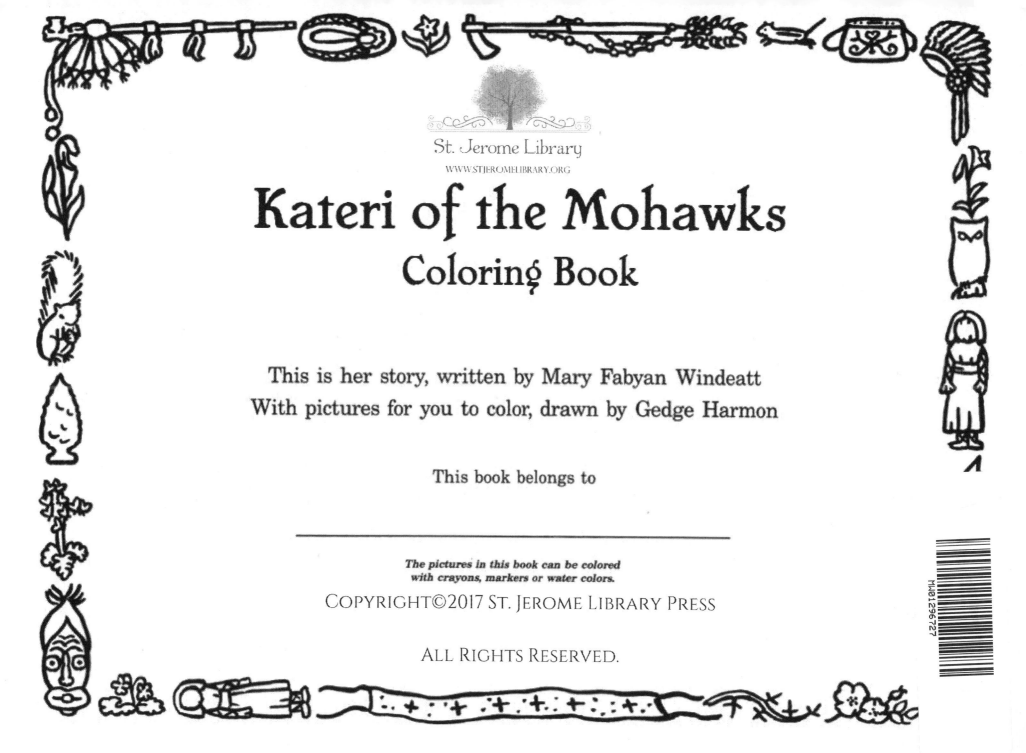

CHAPTER ONE

IT was a chill October night in the year 1660. On the outskirts of the Indian village of Os-ser-ne-non (some forty miles west of the present-day city of Albany, New York), a fifty-year-old Mohawk squaw stood silent and sorrowing. Once again the dread smallpox had struck! Once again the moans of the sick and dying were heard throughout the night!

"Help us, Great White Spirit!" she pleaded. "Save us from the Evil One!"

Yet even as she prayed, Anastasia Te-gon-hat-si-hon-go sensed the malice all about her. She and her fellow-Christians were held to blame for this calamity. Years ago they had embraced the religion of the Blackrobes from Canada, and now the gods were angry.

"Traitor!" hissed a giant brave as he came staggering from the forest, weak with fever. "You have done this to us...."

Anastasia gazed stonily ahead. But a moment later, when the medicine men began their frenzied dance about the campfire in order to appease the gods of misfortune, she slipped from the shadows and hurried off to the main cabin in the village. Perhaps the chief, his Christian wife and two small children would take a turn for the better. Perhaps Ra-wen-ni-o, the Great White Spirit, would yet hear her prayers in their behalf.

CHAPTER TWO

ALAS for Anastasia's hopes! That very night death claimed the chief, his wife and infant son. Even the four-year-old daughter seemed to be breathing her last. But when, in the morning, the tiny sufferer was still clinging to life, Anastasia's spirits rose. Surely the little girl would live?

"Let me bring the small one back to health!" she begged Io-we-ra-no, the child's uncle, who had now succeeded as village chief.

Io-we-ra-no puffed stolidly at his pipe. He had little use for Christians, either squaws or braves, but this Anastasia was a skilled nurse. It could be, with her knowledge of healing roots—

"See to it," he grunted.

Promptly Anastasia began her work. Well she knew what lay behind the childless chief's decision. If his young niece were saved from death, some day a valiant brave would claim her in marriage. Then, according to the Mohawk custom, the youth would come to live in Io-we-ra-no's own cabin and provide him with an endless variety of skins, furs and meat. He would be a son, so to speak, a staff for the chief's old age.

"Open your eyes, little one," crooned Anastasia, as she brought a nourishing drink for the four-year-old, now stirring feebly on her mat. "The sun shines again!"

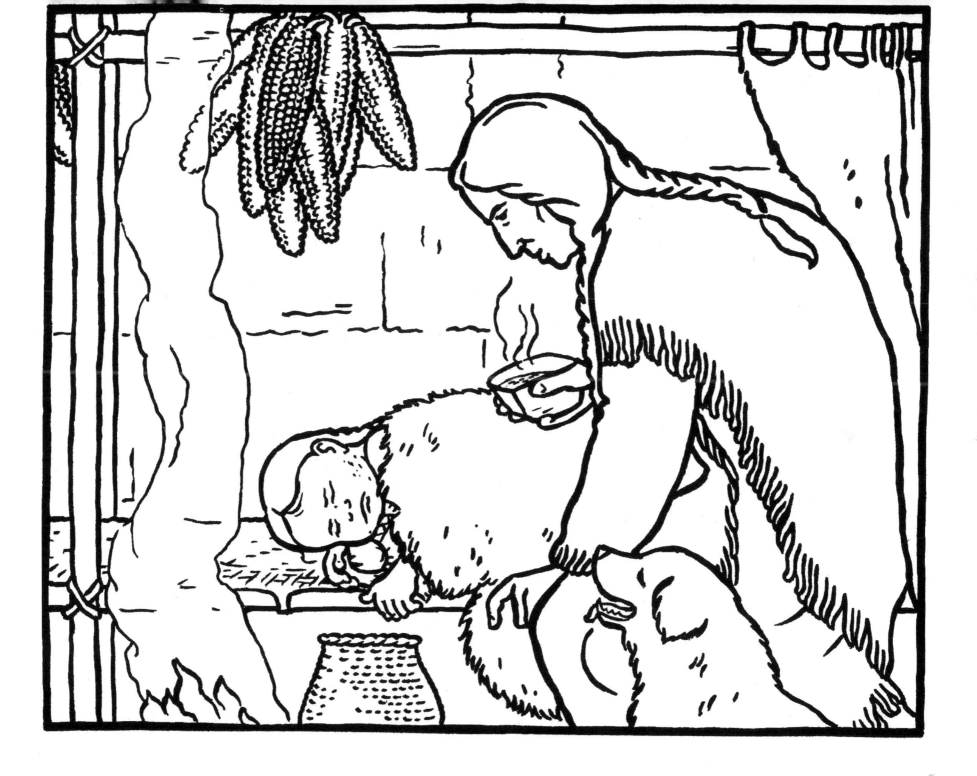

CHAPTER THREE

WITH Anastasia's loving care, the helpless orphan finally regained her strength. But no soothing herbs could remove the deep pock marks from her small face, or undo the damage to her eyes wrought by her illness. In fact, she was now half blind, and never ventured far from home without a stick in her hand. Hence, she came to be known as Tek-ak-with-a—"the one who moves all things before her."

Despite her poor vision, little Tek-ak-with-a became highly skilled at beadwork and the dressing of skins. By the time she was eight, her chieftain-uncle was extremely proud of her, and so were her two aunts. As for Anastasia, she constantly prayed that some day a visiting Blackrobe would baptize the clever little girl. Io-we-ra-no would object, of course, but if the priest were as strong and fearless as the missionaries who had come before him. . . .

One day, as she and Tek-ak-with-a were gathering wood in the forest, she voiced this thought. "Oh, he will be!" cried the child joyfully. "The Blackrobe will come before another moon has passed. Twelve moons later he will pour the blessed water on my head. Then I shall be like my mother."

Anastasia smiled, but her eyes were troubled. "Such foolish chatter, little one! Have I not said the trees have ears? We must watch our words."

But even as she spoke, Io-we-ra-no was standing before them, tall and forbidding. "Enough!" he snapped. "To the cabin!"

CHAPTER FOUR

THAT night the little girl cried herself to sleep. How angry her uncle had been with her, and with Anastasia, too, because of their love for the Great White Spirit! And to think that she might never belong to Ra-wen-ni-io, even if the Blackrobe did come—

"It's all I want!" she sobbed the next morning. "It's all I'll ever want. . . ."

Her two aunts glared. What a disgrace that the daughter of a Mohawk chief should want to be a Christian! Couldn't she realize that the white man was an enemy? That he had come from France, far across the Big Water, only to make trouble for the Indians? To seize their lands and ruin their hunting? No decent Indian girl should want to worship in his fashion.

Tek-ak-with-a's lips trembled. "But if my mother was a Christian—"

"Your mother was a nobody, little fool, a stupid Algonquin from Canada whom your father took captive at Three Rivers and treated better than she deserved."

"But Anastasia says—"

"Another Christian dog! You will speak to her no more."

Suddenly Tek-ak-with-a began to cry as though her heart would break. How could she live without Anastasia, her best friend in all the world?

"O Great White Spirit, help me!" she sobbed. "Hear what I have to say. . . ."

CHAPTER FIVE

A FEW months later Tek-ak-with-a began to guard her tongue. Since Io-we-ra-no had given her a home and the two aunts loved her in their own fashion, it did not seem right to hurt their feelings by any further reference to the Great White Spirit. Rather, she must repay their kindness by working long and hard at whatever tasks they gave her. And she must try to keep away from Anastasia, too.

"A good girl after all," grunted Io-we-ra-no approvingly.

The aunts smiled and nodded. "A good girl," they said.

Tek-ak-with-a was happy that the family was pleased with her. Yet what about the future? In a few years she would be expected to marry. And though marriage was fine and honorable in itself, she wanted no part of it. Deep in her heart was the feeling that the Great White Spirit had other plans for her, although what these might be she could not guess.

In the summer of 1667, when Tek-ak-with-a was eleven, there was great excitement in the village. After years of bloodshed, peace had finally been declared between the Indian and the white man, and now three Blackrobes had just arrived from Canada. Since they bore greetings from the Governor in Quebec, they must be honorably received and allowed to minister to all the Christians whom the Mohawks had taken captive through the years.

The little girl's heart beat fast at the news. "If I speak to the Blackrobes, perhaps they will help me, too," she decided.

CHAPTER SIX

ALAS for Tek-ak-with-a's hopes! During the missionaries' three-day stay in the village, she sensed that her family's hatred of the white man was just as strong as ever. Peace had been declared, of course, and so the visitors must not be harmed, but what scoundrels they actually were! Only a fool would believe their talk of Ra-wen-ni-io, the Great White Spirit Who had died on a cross, and Who wanted all men to live as brothers.

Gradually Tek-ak-with-a's courage began to fail. Her uncle would be terribly angry if she spoke in secret to the Blackrobes. As for the Blackrobes themselves—suppose they made fun of her, a half-blind little Indian girl with a pock-marked face?

"No, I won't talk to them," she decided.

But in the months following the missionaries' departure, Tek-ak-with-a bitterly regretted her lack of spirit. Surely the Blackrobes were wise and kind and good? Surely they would have been glad to help her, perhaps even to explain her strange aversion to marriage?

"I was a fool," she muttered. "O Great White Spirit, forgive me!"

Then one night in the year 1669, shortly after her thirteenth birthday, Tek-ak-with-a's aunts smilingly insisted that she change into her best clothes. A fine young brave had come with his family for supper, they said. She must help to make the guests feel at home.

CHAPTER SEVEN

TEK-AK-WITH-A obeyed without misgiving. Clad in her best dress, bright with embroidery and beadwork, her black hair bound in scarlet eelskin, she chatted pleasantly with the visitors. But when, at suppertime, one of the aunts playfully put a bowl of ground corn into her hands, she was startled into silence. Why, if she offered this particular food to the young brave sitting beside her (as all the rules of hospitality demanded), the Mohawk law would consider her to be his wife!

"No, no!" she burst out, after a moment. "I can't do it!" And dropping the bowl, she sprang to her feet and sped from the cabin like a hunted wild thing.

Upon her return, hours later, she found Io-we-ra-no and the aunts furious. Was this the way Tek-ak-with-a repaid all their kindness and hospitality? Why, the young brave and his family had been insulted beyond repair by her rudeness! How dared she neglect her duty of bringing a fine son-in-law into the cabin so that her uncle might take things easier in his old age?

The thirteen-year-old hung her head. "I . . . I really don't want to marry," she stammered.

Unmoved by any threat or plea, Tek-ak-with-a persevered in her resolution not to take a husband. Her nineteenth birthday found her still unmarried. And in another way, too, she refused to conform to the custom of the tribe. She could not be prevailed upon to watch the torture of captives.

"It's not right," she said tearfully. "The Great White Spirit doesn't like it."

CHAPTER EIGHT

DISGUSTED with her behavior, the uncle and aunts now treated Tek-ak-with-a with the contempt due to one who had failed her tribe. Her weak eyes suffered from the sunlight, did they? No matter. She would labor all summer in the fields. She was frail and under-sized? Chopping wood in the forest and dragging it home, load by load, would make her husky enough.

The nineteen-year-old girl did not dream of complaining, although it was hard not to think of happier days. Ah, if only Anastasia were here, the kindly friend of her childhood! If only they might talk together about Ra-wen-ni-io! But Anastasia had recently gone to live at Sault Saint Louis, a village for Christian Indians which the Blackrobes had founded near the Canadian city of Montreal. There was little hope that she would ever see her again.

One day late in the summer of 1675, Tek-ak-with-a sat at home weaving baskets. An injured foot had kept her from her work in the fields. All was peaceful, for her uncle and aunts were away and only two old neighbor women dozed by the fire. Suddenly a strange figure paused briefly before the open door of the cabin. The girl looked into his face and her heart almost stopped beating. It was a Blackrobe!

"Father!" she cried, struggling painfully to rise. "W-won't you c-come in?"

CHAPTER NINE

FATHER James de Lamberville stared in amazement. Newcomer though he was, he had heard of Io-we-ra-no's hatred of the True Faith and so had decided to visit only the Christian captives in the village—a privilege permitted by the present peace treaty between the Indians and the French. But now, at the sight of the chief's eager-faced niece—

"Of course," he said cheerfully. "What can I do for you, child?"

Tek-ak-with-a's heart pounded with excitement. There was so little time before the family would return! "I . . . I want to be baptized!" she burst out. "I want to belong to Ra-wen-ni-io!"

The priest hesitated. How could he give this girl any spiritual help when her uncle was so bitterly opposed to the True Faith? Yet Tek-ak-with-a pleaded her cause so earnestly, insisting she would bear any suffering if only some day the blessed water might be poured on her head, that there and then he began her instruction.

Surprisingly enough, Io-we-ra-no merely shrugged when he heard the news. The aunts, too, were unmoved. Tek-ak-with-a had long been a disgrace to the family. What did it matter now if she were one with the Christian dogs? Thus, eight months later, on Easter Sunday, April 18 1676, in the tiny bark chapel of the Christian captives, Tek-ak-with-a's heart all but burst for joy. She, a poor Mohawk girl of twenty years, was about to receive the great Sacrament of Baptism!

CHAPTER TEN

TEK-AK-WITH-A'S new Christian name was Catherine; or, as the Indians called the famous saint of Alexandria, Kateri. And how the girl loved to hear about this youthful patroness who had suffered martyrdom rather than worship false gods!

"Perhaps the good saint will help our little convert to destroy the false gods of the Indian," mused Father de Lamberville one day. "How wonderful that would be!" Yet even as the thought crossed his mind, the priest's heart grew heavy. For many years Kateri had undergone severe hardships at the hands of her uncle and aunts. But now that she was a Christian, things were far worse. Despite her heavy labors, she was allowed scarcely enough to eat. And there was endless nagging and scolding at home, no matter how earnestly she strove to please.

"Kateri ought to go to Sault Saint Louis," decided the priest finally. "Anastasia would love to have her, and there'd be peace for the girl at last."

Late in the year 1677, Father de Lamberville became gravely concerned for Kateri's well-being. Realizing that it would be impossible to obtain Io-we-ra-no's consent to her release, he arranged for her to escape to Canada with two Indians visiting from the Sault. God willing, the perilous journey would be made without mishap.

CHAPTER ELEVEN

IT was in the darkness before dawn of a November day that the little group finally slipped away. As their canoe glided through the chill waters of the Mohawk river, Kateri and her two guides scarcely dared to breathe. Suppose their departure had been noticed? It was many miles to the Lake of the Blessed Sacrament (which some day white men would rename Lake George), and even farther to Lake Champlain and the winding trail that led to the safety of the Christian village near the city of Montreal.

"Help us, Great White Spirit!" they pleaded. "Be with us on our way!"

The fervent prayers were answered. No harm came to the travelers in the wilderness of stream and forest. And when they finally reached Sault Saint Louis, they found the entire village eager to greet them.

"Welcome! A thousand welcomes!" cried Anastasia, pressing the exhausted Kateri to her heart.

Tears of joy filled the girl's eyes as she returned her good friend's embrace. How wonderful to be loved and wanted! To know that in this new home she might serve Ra-wen-ni-io in peace! Then, as she glimpsed a smiling Blackrobe standing near, she fumbled for the small sealed envelope which Father de Lamberville had given to her.

"For you, Father," she said shyly, and dropped to her knees.

CHAPTER TWELVE

FATHER Cholonec glanced curiously at the contents of the envelope. "Kateri Tek-ak-with-a is going to live at the Sault," ran a brief note in Father de Lamberville's handwriting. "Will you kindly undertake to direct her? You will soon know what a treasure we have sent you. Guard it well. May it profit in your hands for the glory of God and the salvation of a soul that is very dear to Him."

Deeply impressed, the missionary replaced the note in its envelope, then blessed the kneeling girl. "Child, I shall do my very best to help you," he said kindly.

Soon Kateri was happier than she had ever been in her whole life. More than five hundred Indians were living at the Sault, of every tribe and nation, and all were trying hard to know, love and serve God. Each morning they heard Mass, listened to an instruction and recited the Rosary. At night they came together again for prayers in common. And over and above all this regular devotion, they practised severe penance for former sins—especially the worship of false gods, drunkenness and the torture of captives.

"Oh, it's so good to be here!" Kateri told herself on Christmas Day, as she knelt before the Crib after having made her First Communion. "Little-One-in-the-Straw, what can I do to thank You?"

CHAPTER THIRTEEN

FATHER Cholonec had an answer for that question. Kateri must work hard, pray hard and always try to remember God's presence in those about her. "Especially when you find that hard to do," he added, smilingly.

The same advice was given another convert, a young widow named Marie Therese Te-ga-ia-guen-ta, who had become Kateri's close friend. However, Marie Therese felt that in her case the priest had been far too lenient. "I've been wicked in the past," she said. "I ought to do some special penance."

Kateri smiled reassuringly. "I ought to do some special penance, too, Marie Therese—for my sins and the sins of my people. Shall we offer a Rosary barefoot in the snow?"

Marie Therese agreed, and soon the two friends had discovered that the more they prayed and sacrificed for love of Ra-wen-ni-io, the happier they were. Then one day Father Cholonec permitted them to join some other Indians who were going to display their handiwork at the marketplace in Montreal. The short trip down the river would do them good, he said, not to mention a visit with the Sisters.

The Sisters? Kateri was puzzled. But soon Marie Therese had explained about the kindly French women who had come to Canada to teach the children and to nurse the sick. One of these, Sister Marguerite Bourgeoys, was surely a saint. "You'll love her, Kateri!" said Marie Therese impulsively. "I just know you will!"

CHAPTER FOURTEEN

A WARM welcome did await the two friends at Sister Bourgeoys' convent school. Also at the Hotel-Dieu, the local hospital. Indeed, for several weeks Kateri could think of nothing else but the holiness of the kindly French ladies whose entire lives were dedicated to Ra-wen-ni-io. Then one day, while gazing at remote Heron Island in the swift waters of the Saint Lawrence—

"Maybe Marie Therese and I could be Sisters, too," she mused. "Maybe we could build a little convent over there on the island...."

Marie Therese was delighted when she heard about the idea, likewise Marie Ska-ri-chi-ons, another young resident of the Sault. But when they confided their plan to Father Cholonec, he merely smiled.

"No, children," he said kindly. "None of you is experienced enough as a Christian to be able to lead the religious life."

Disappointed, the three said no more. But on March 25, 1679, when she had been at the Sault for some sixteen months, Father Cholonec did permit Kateri to make a private vow of virginity—a promise to God that since she loved Him above all creatures, she would remain unmarried.

"Never before has an Indian girl wanted to do such a thing," the priest reflected in amazement. "Ah, how God must love our little Kateri to send her such a grace!"

Page Twenty-Eight

BLESSED KATERI TEKAKWITHA

CHAPTER FIFTEEN

AS the months passed, however, Marie Therese began to worry about Kateri's health. Through constant fasting the girl had become little more than skin and bones. As for the terrible cough that racked her whole body—

"You mustn't do penance any more," she declared one day. "It's not right."

Kateri tried to smile. "Don't worry, Marie Therese. Nothing's wrong with me. I'm just a little tired, that's all."

"Tired! And why not, when you've been lying on sharp thorns night after night?"

"Please! That's to make up for my sins . . . and the sins of my people. . . ."

However, in February, 1680, Kateri finally agreed to give a complete account of her mortifications to Father Cholonec, who was shocked beyond words when he heard it. "God doesn't want you to kill yourself, child!" he exclaimed. "Why didn't you ask permission for such things?"

Kateri hesitated. "I . . . I didn't think it was necessary, Father. Besides, I wanted so much to do something for souls. . . ."

The priest nodded sympathetically, but his heart was troubled as he looked at the twenty-four-year-old girl. Why, she scarcely had the strength to stand, let alone work long hours in the cold and damp—

"All right, child," he said finally. "But from now on you're to take the best possible care of yourself. Understand?"

Kateri smiled. "Yes, Father. I understand."

CHAPTER SIXTEEN

TWO months later, however, everyone at Sault Saint Louis knew that Kateri Tek-ak-with-a was sick unto death.

"It's all my fault!" sobbed Maria Therese bitterly. "I should never have talked to her about doing penance—"

Kateri hastened to comfort her good friend. "No, no!" she whispered. "Never give up mortification! Take courage . . . I will love you in heaven . . . I will pray for you. . . ."

On April 17, the Wednesday of Holy Week, 1680, a sorrowing little group gathered in Kateri's cabin. It was three o'clock in the afternoon, and the end had just come. But as Maria Therese knelt weeping beside the body of her dead friend, her heartbeats quickened. Suddenly the ugly pock marks had vanished from Kateri's face, and she was incredibly radiant and lovely. Could it really be possible—

"Yes, child," said Father Cholonec gently, reading her excited thoughts. "I'm sure that Kateri is now a saint in heaven."

Soon countless others were of like mind. What favors "The Lily of the Mohawks" was showering on those who asked her help! What miracles of healing! Through the centuries the favors continued, and then, on June 12, 1942, the voice of Pope Pius the Twelfth joined the chorus of praise. Yes, Kateri Tek-ak-with-a had lived and died in the practice of heroic virtue. She was truly a Venerable Servant of God.

Windeatt Coloring Book Series Titles

Vol. 1 St. Teresa of Avila
Vol. 2 St. Pius X
Vol. 3 St. Philomena
Vol. 4 St. Meinrad
Vol. 5 St. Maria Goretti
Vol. 6 Kateri of the Mohawks
Vol 7 St. Joan of Arc
Vol. 8 St. Francis of Assisi
Vol. 9 St. Frances Cabrini
Vol. 10 St. Dominic Savio
Vol. 11 St. Christopher
Vol. 12 St. Anthony of Padua

Vol. 13 Our Lady of Banneux
Vol. 14 Our Lady of Beuraing
Vol. 15 Our Lady of Fatima
Vol. 16 Our Lady of Guadalupe
Vol. 17 Our Lady of Knock
Vol. 18 Our Lady of La Salette
Vol. 19 Our Lady of Lourdes
Vol. 20 Our Lady of the Miraculous Medal
Vol. 21 Our Lady of Pellevoisin
Vol. 22 Our Lady of Pontmain

Vol. 23 The Brown Scapular
Vol. 24 The Rosary

Made in the USA
Las Vegas, NV
24 June 2024